MYSTIC FOREST of CHI

Coloring Book For Adults

Fantasy Art Coloring Book For Stress Relief

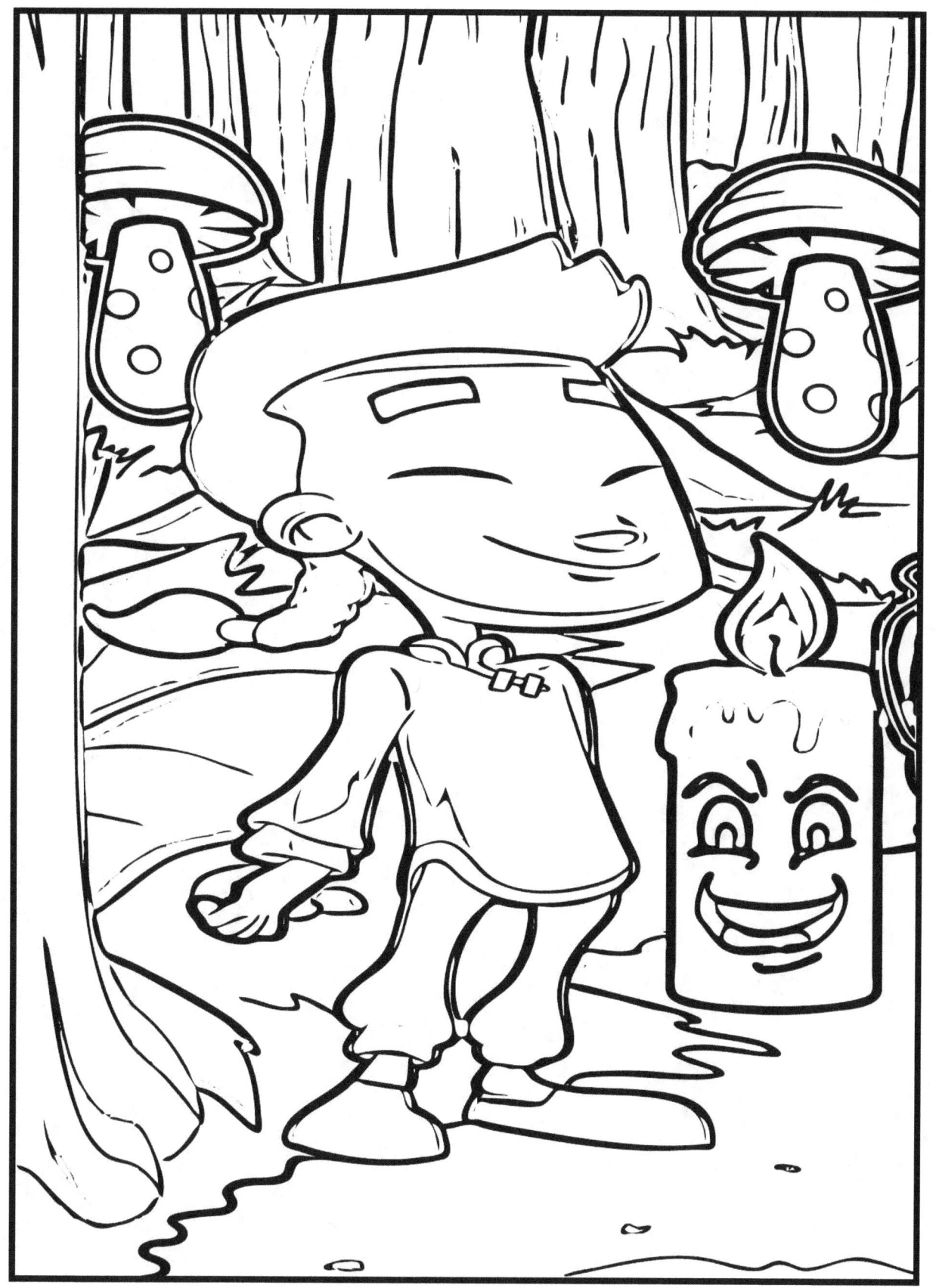

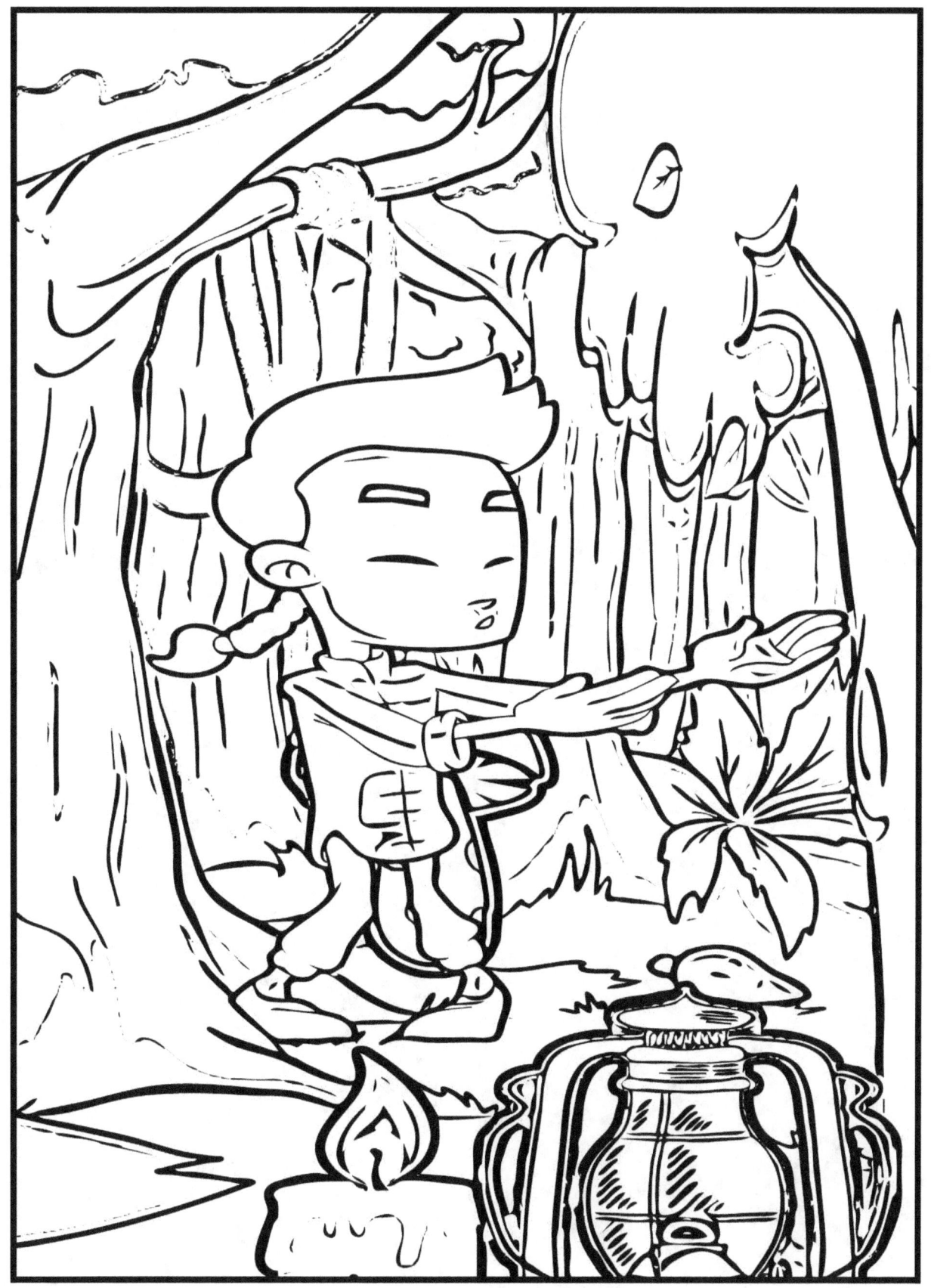

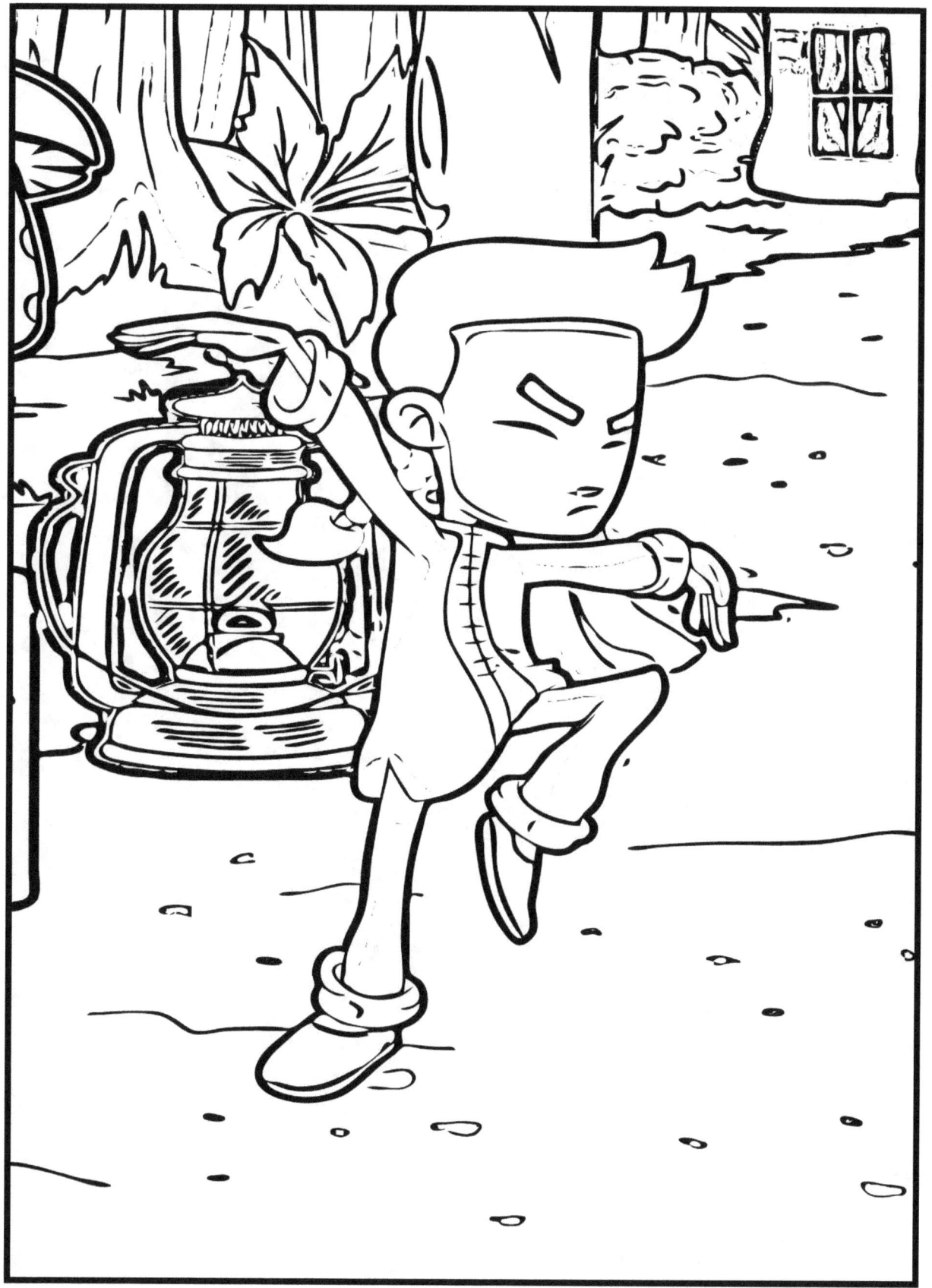

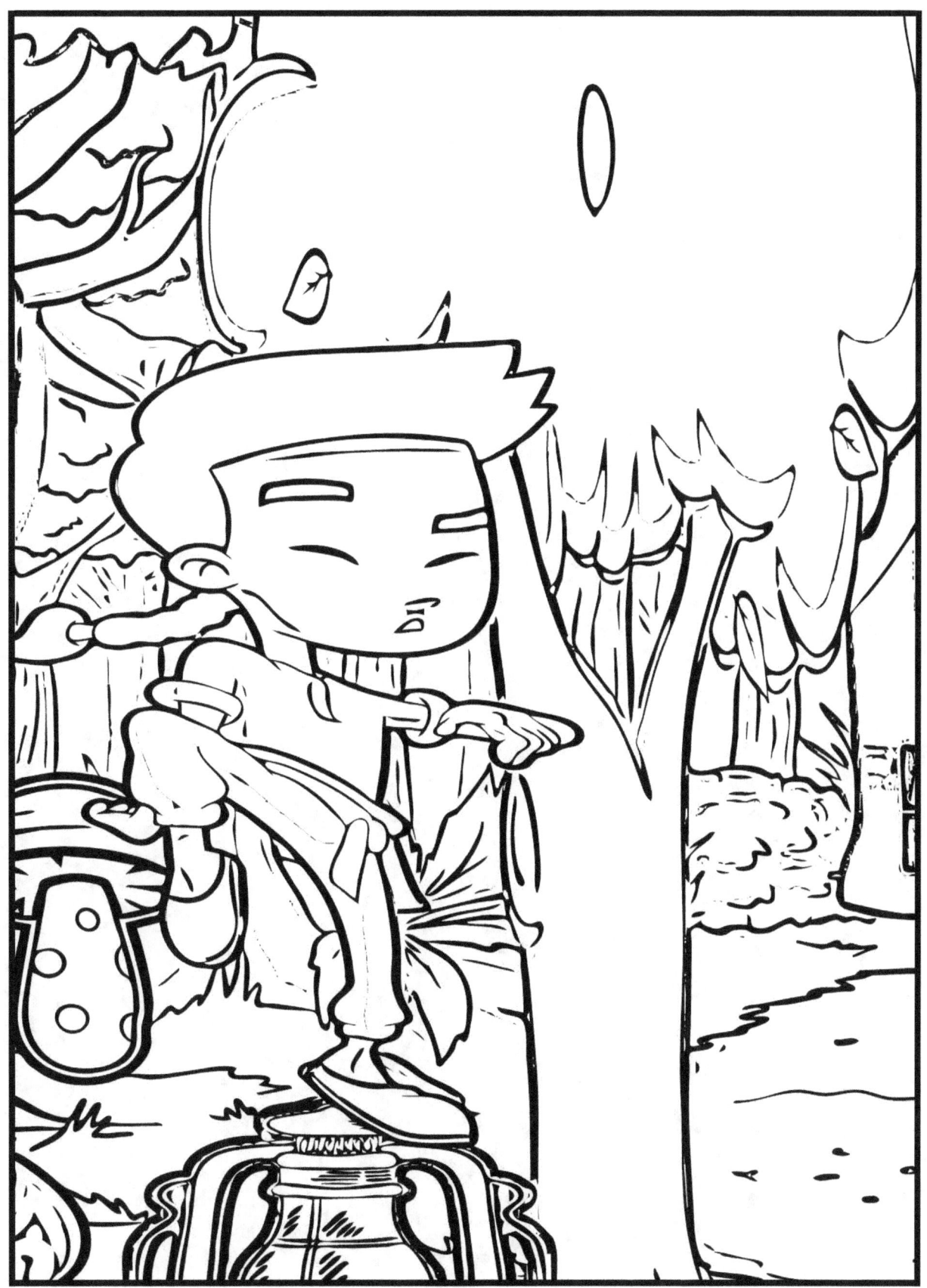

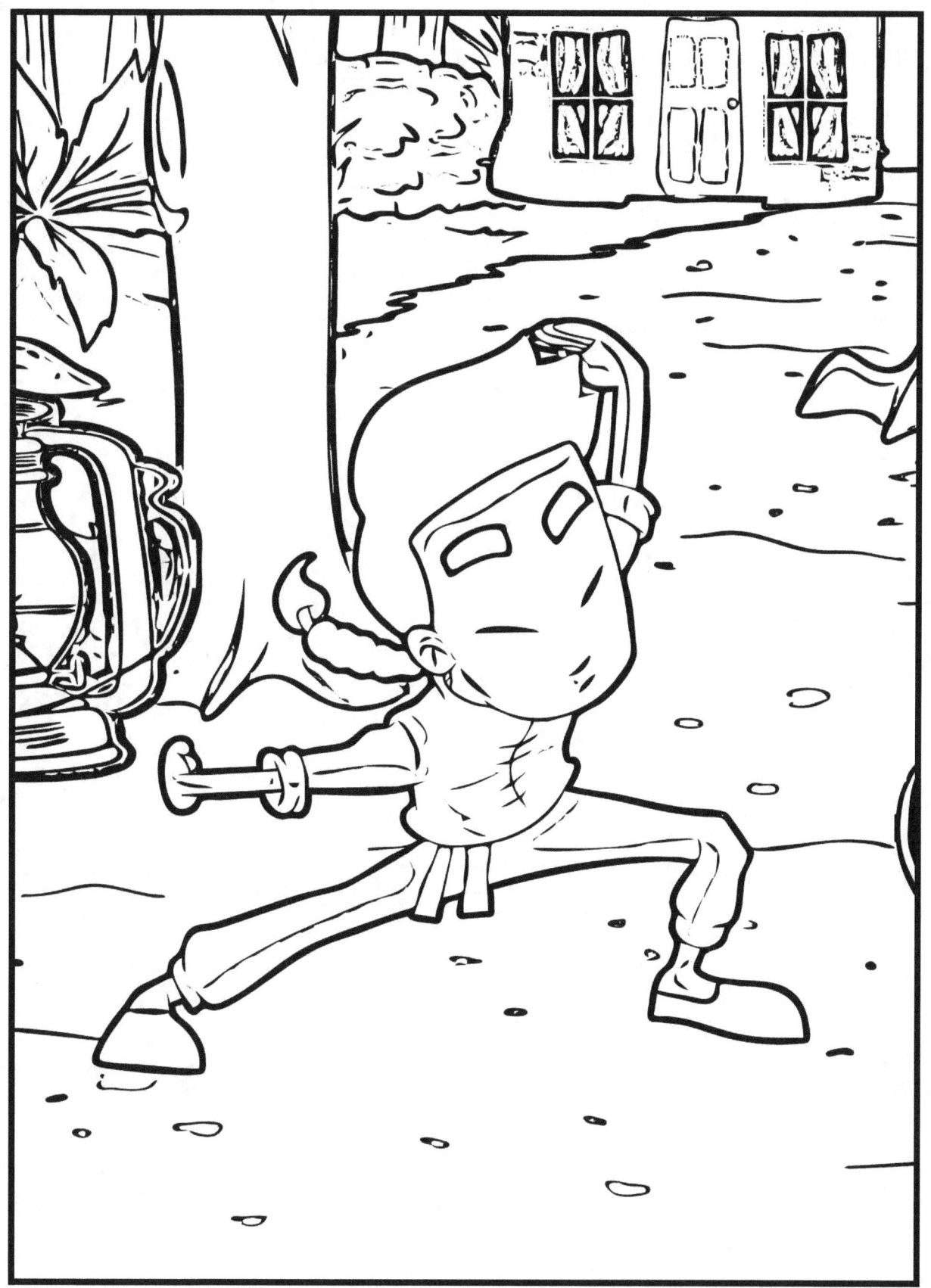

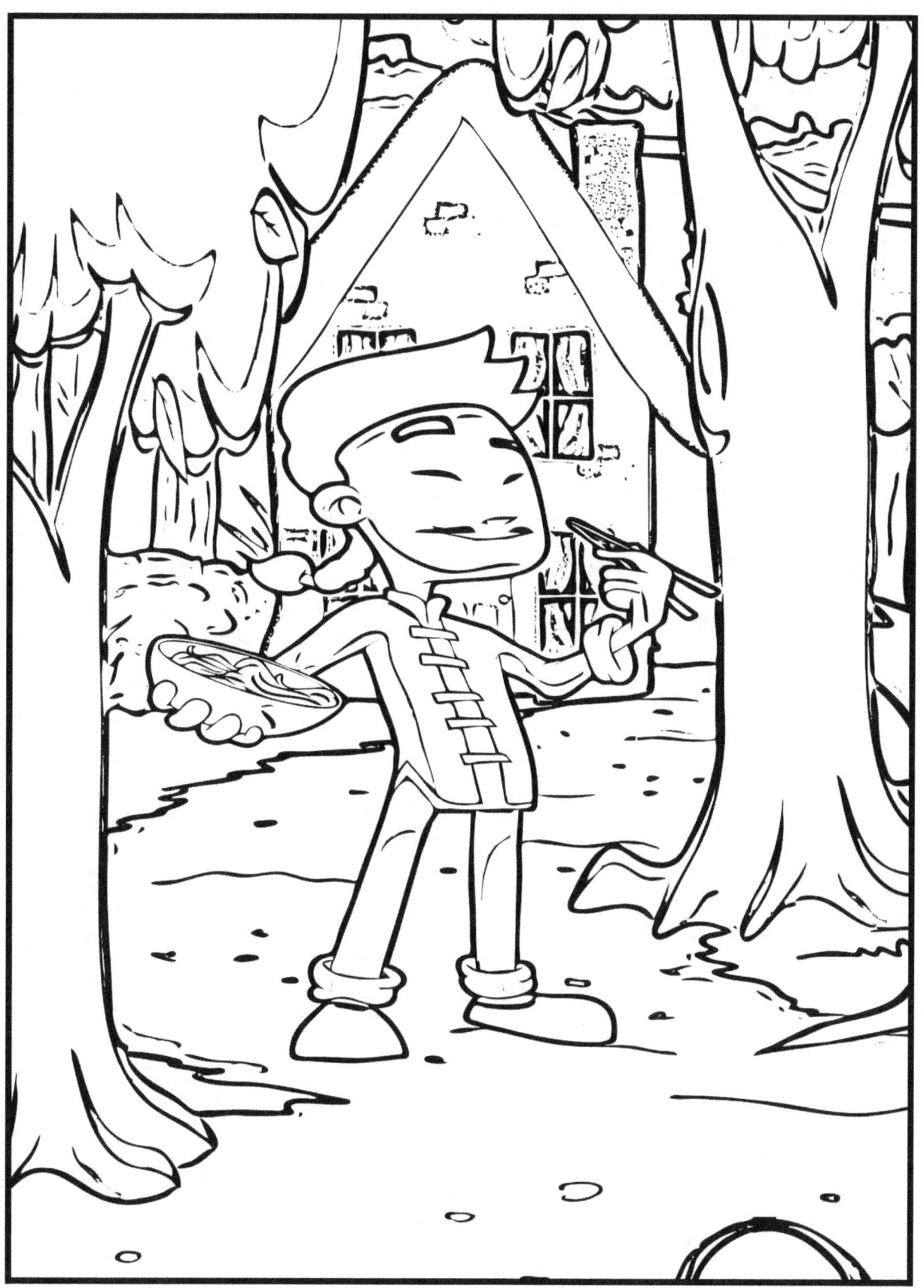

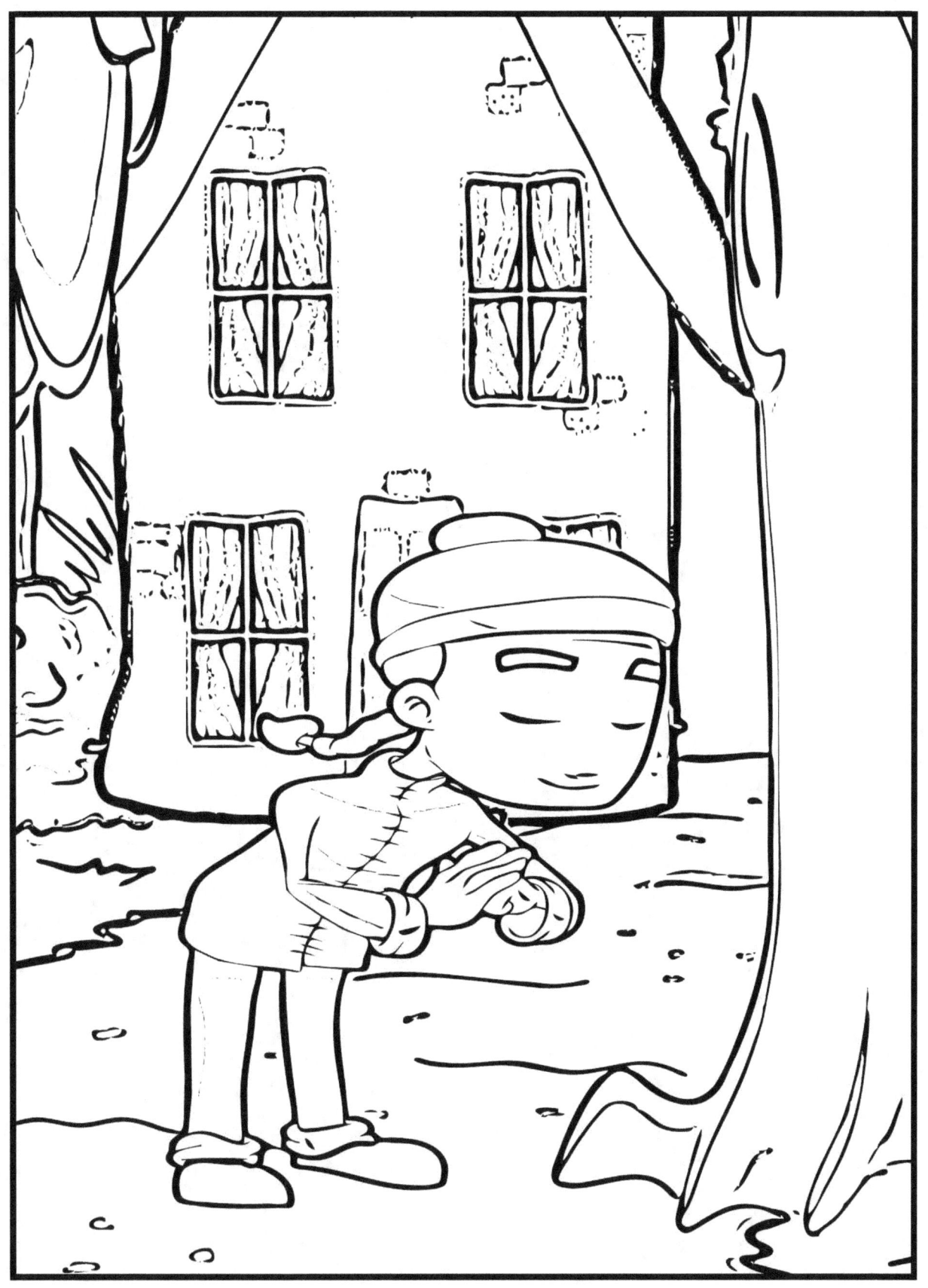

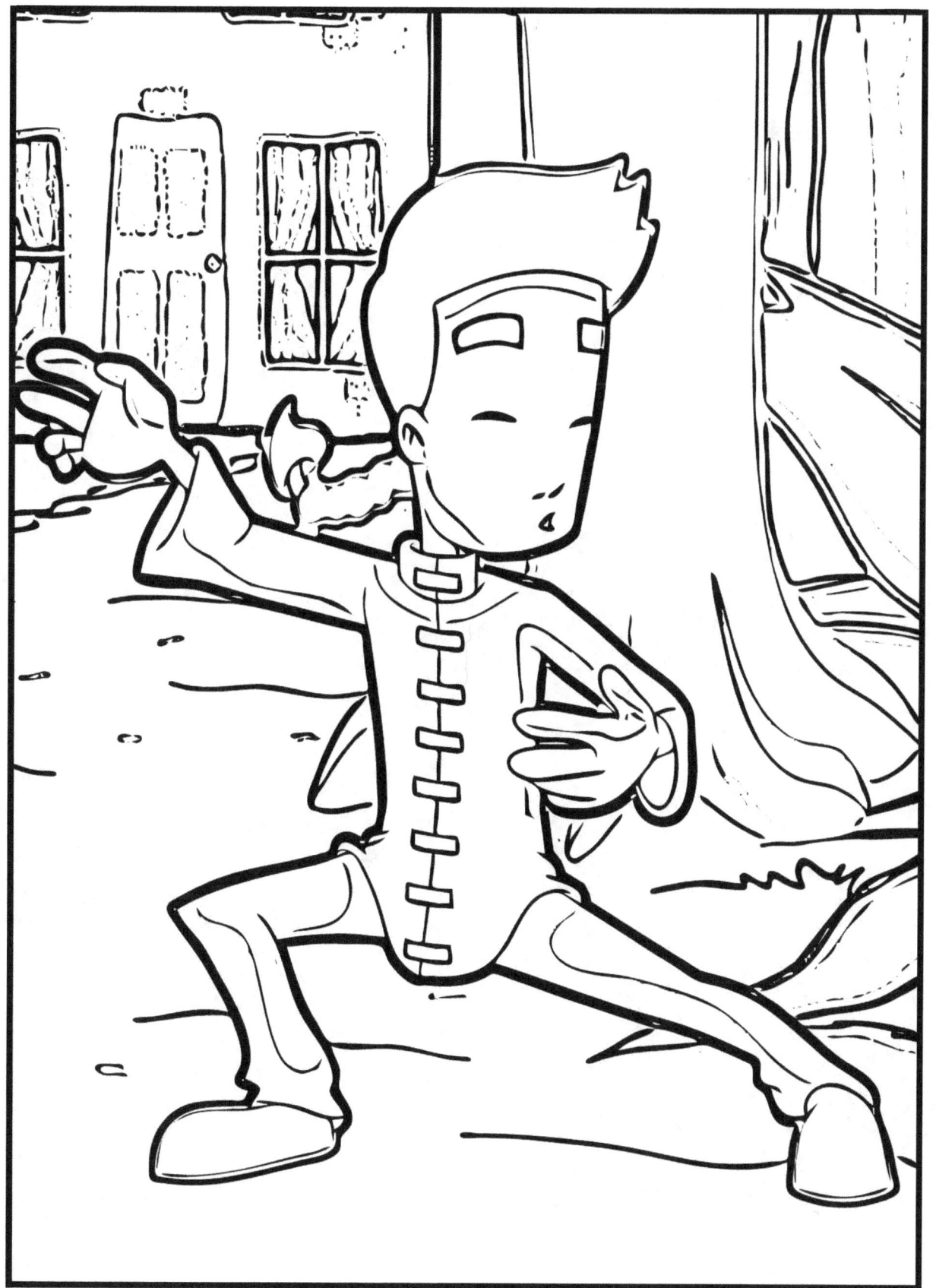

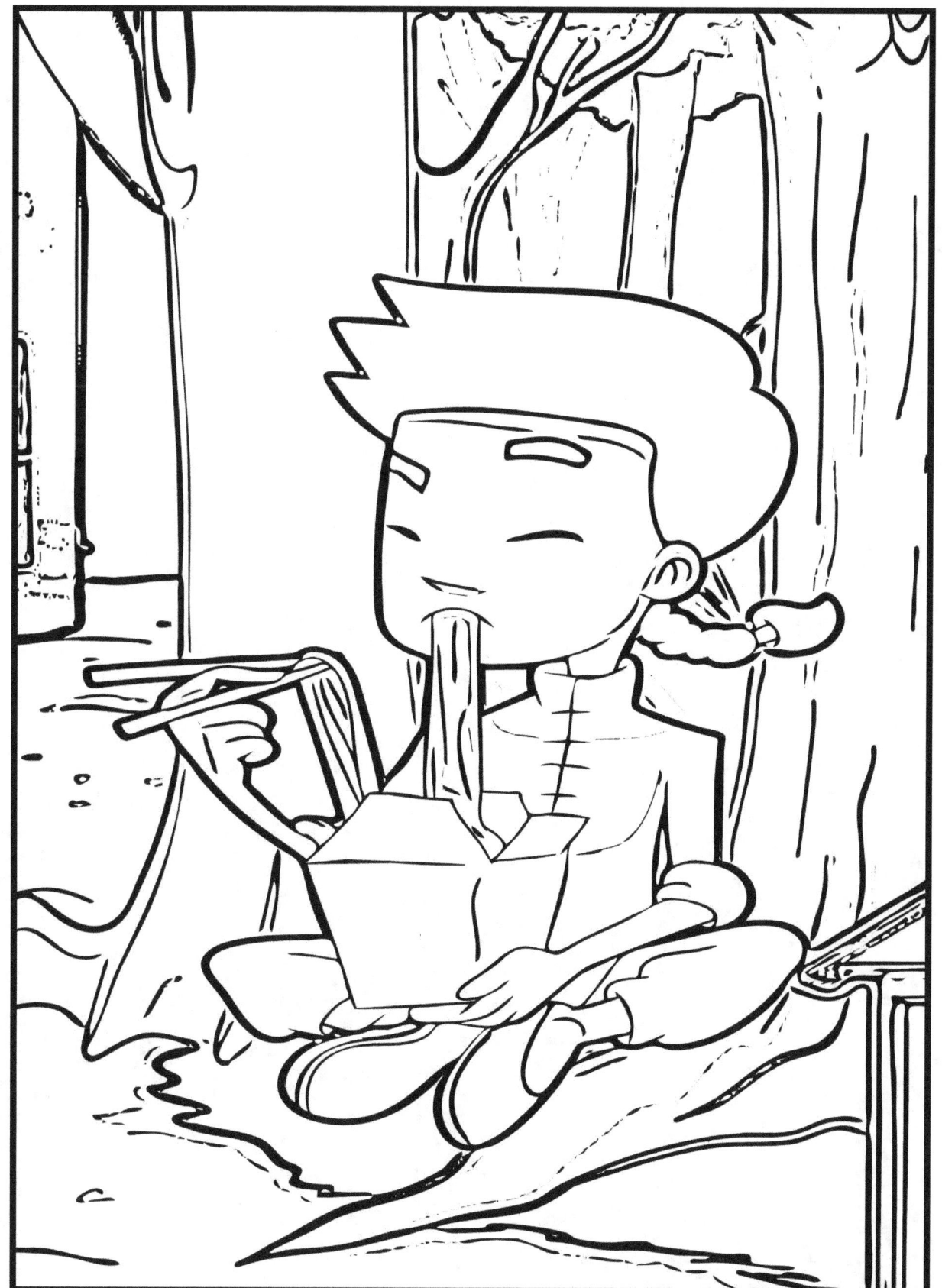

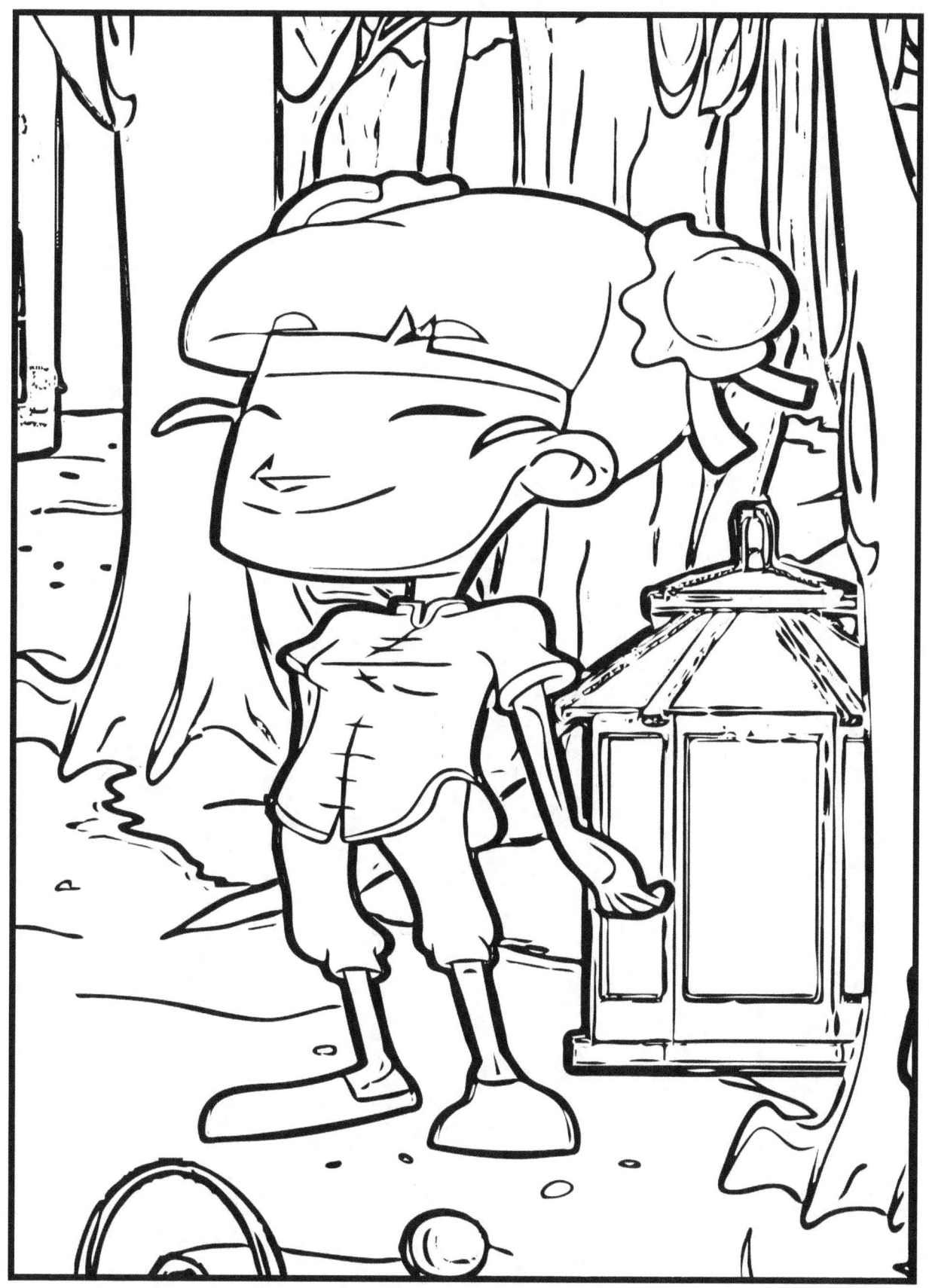

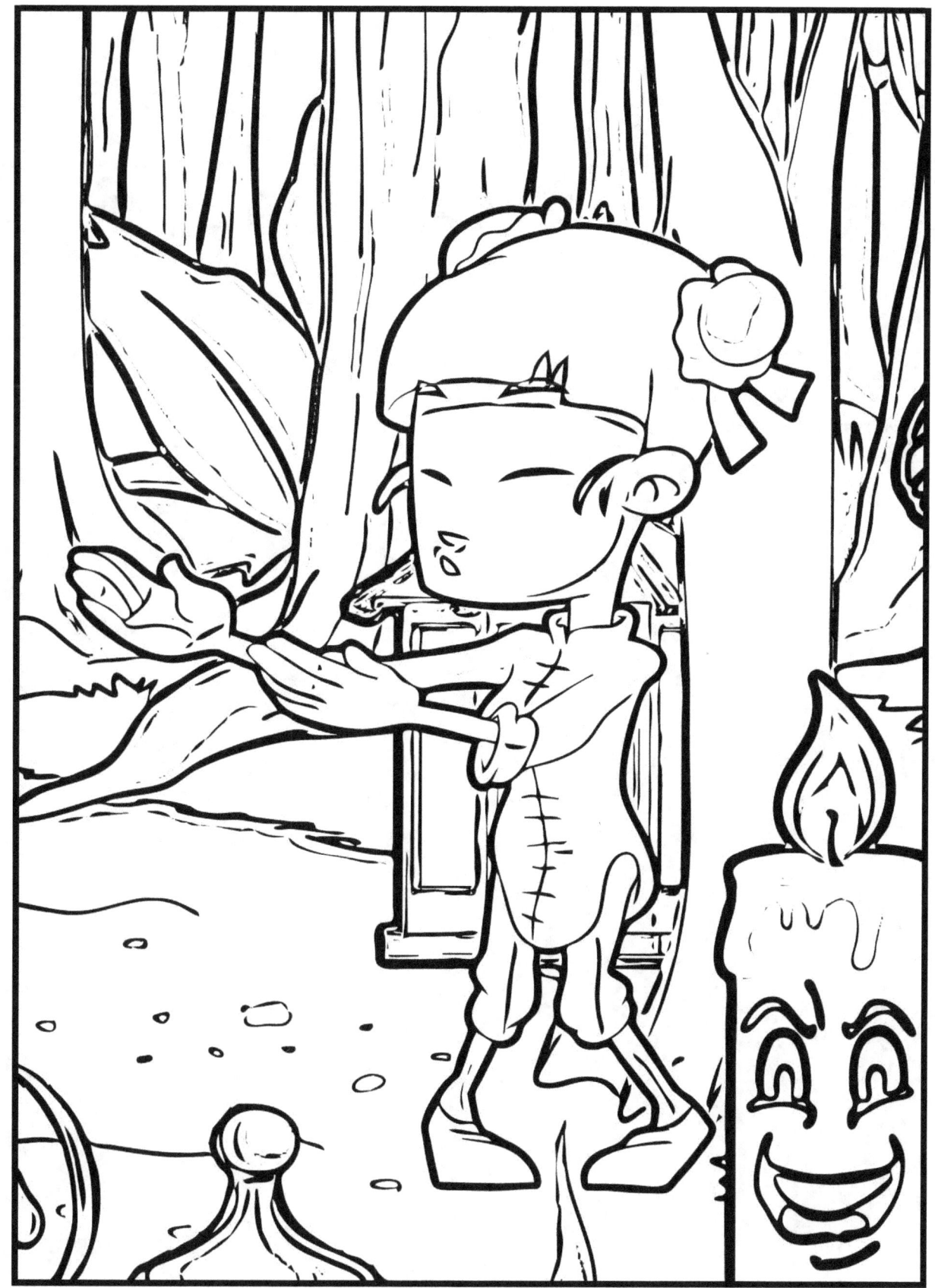

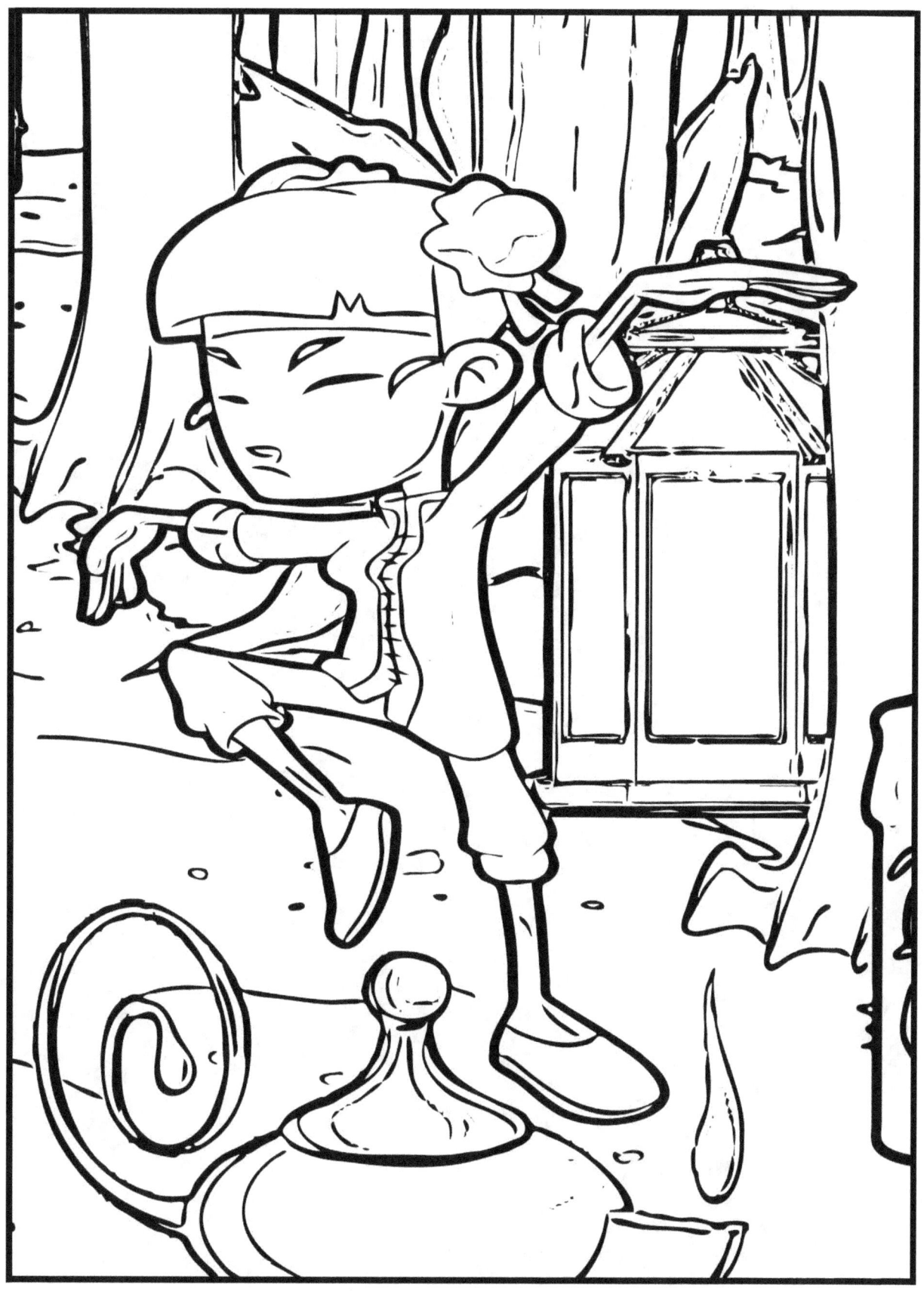

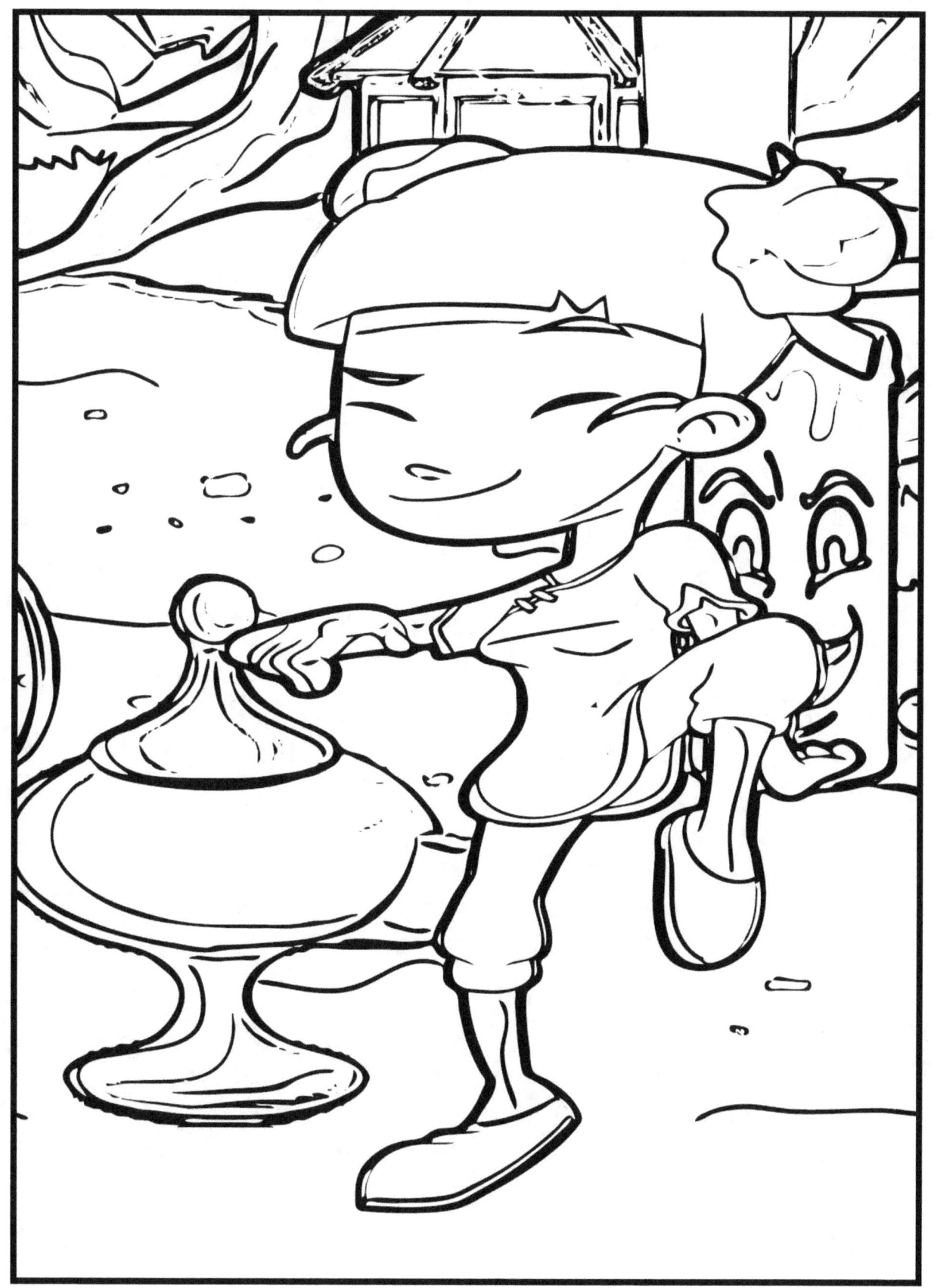

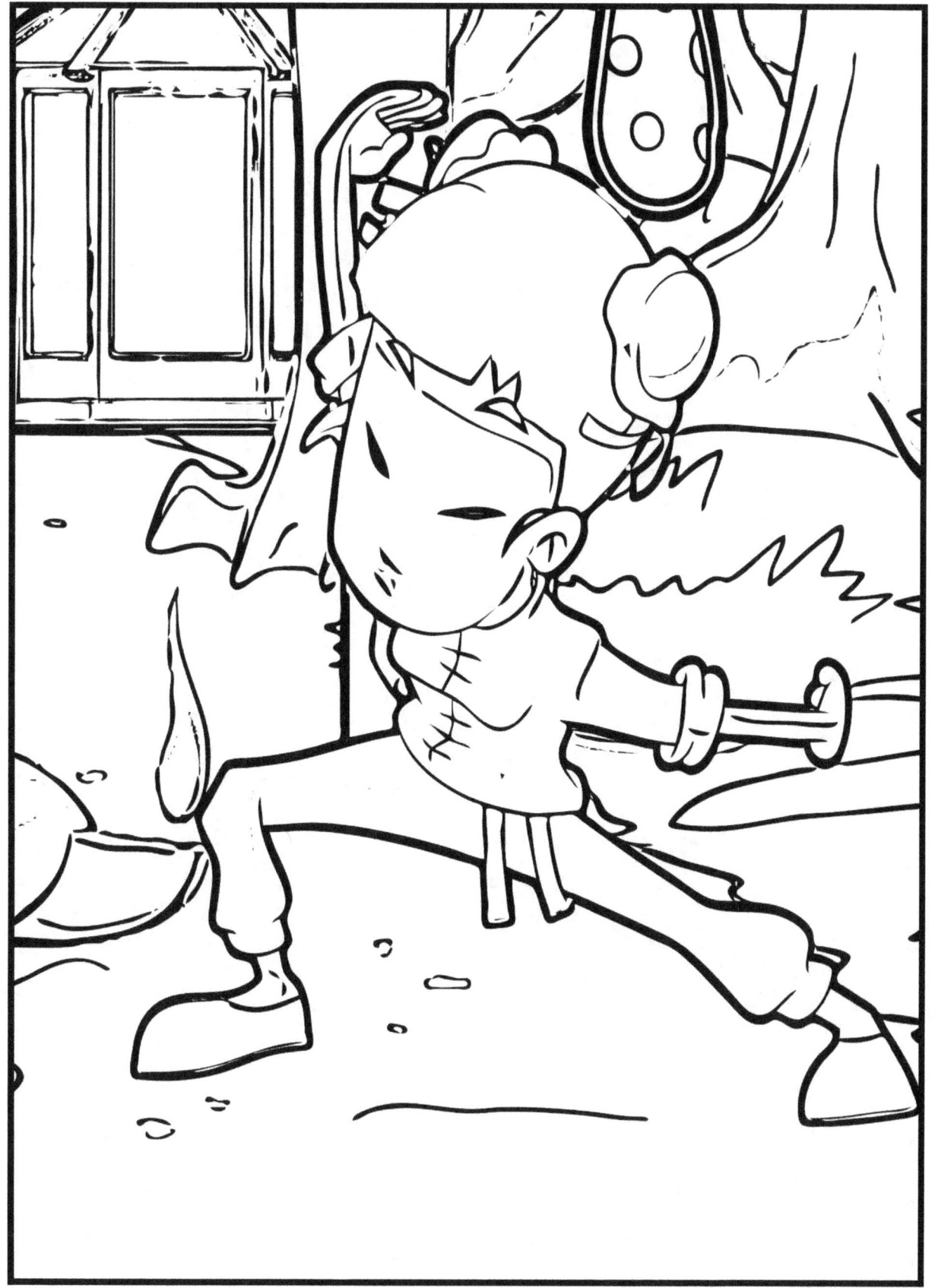

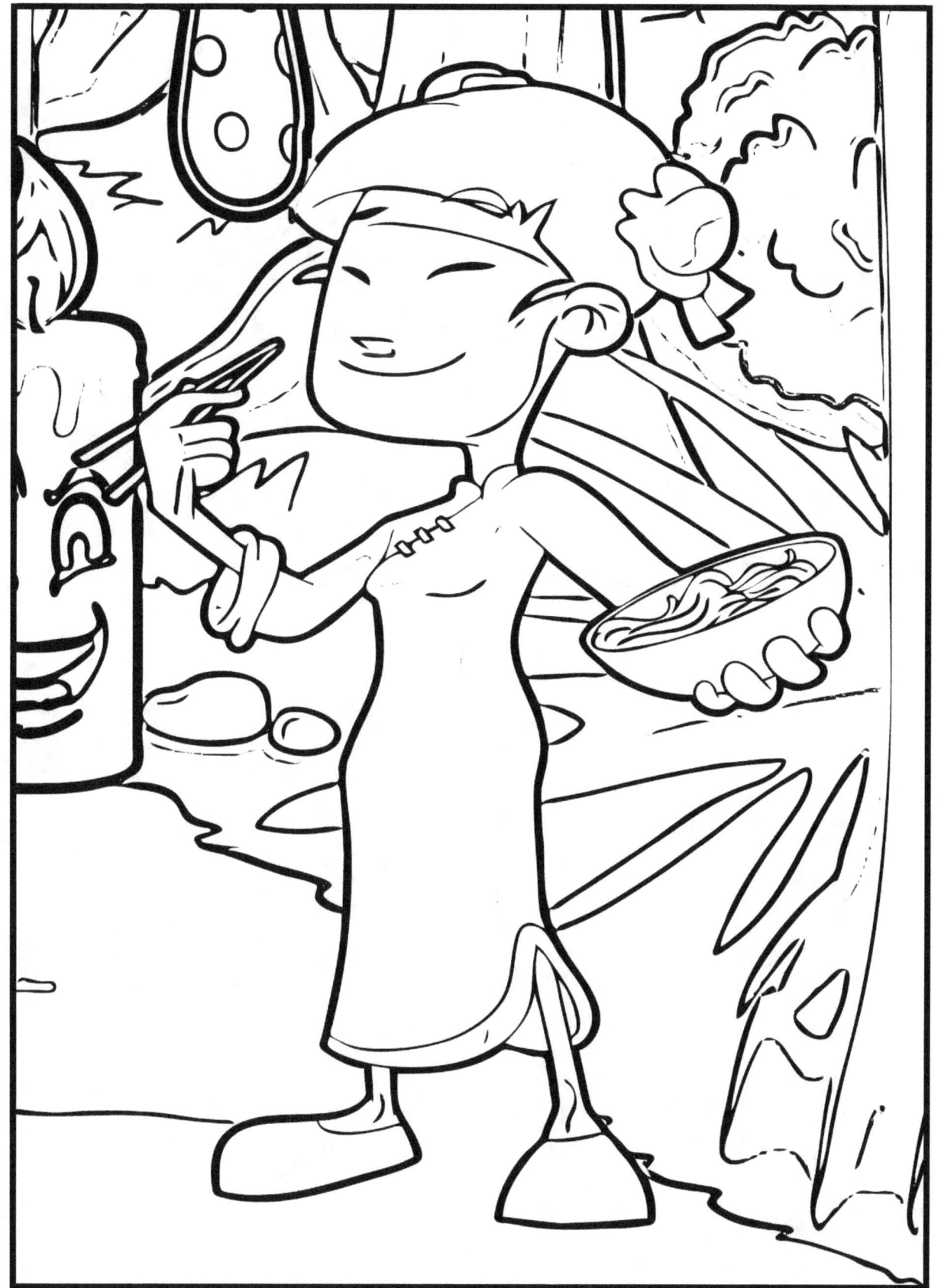

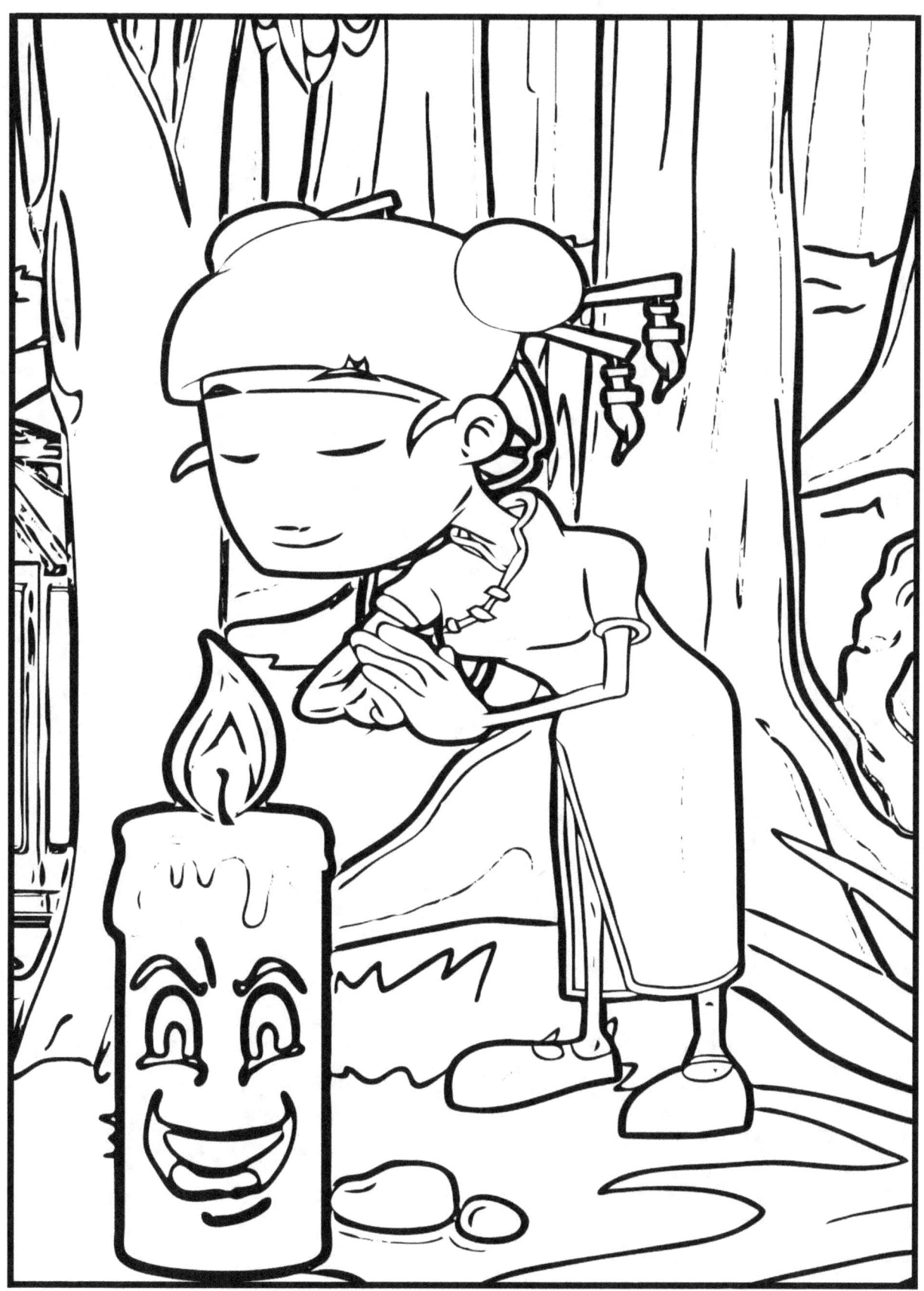

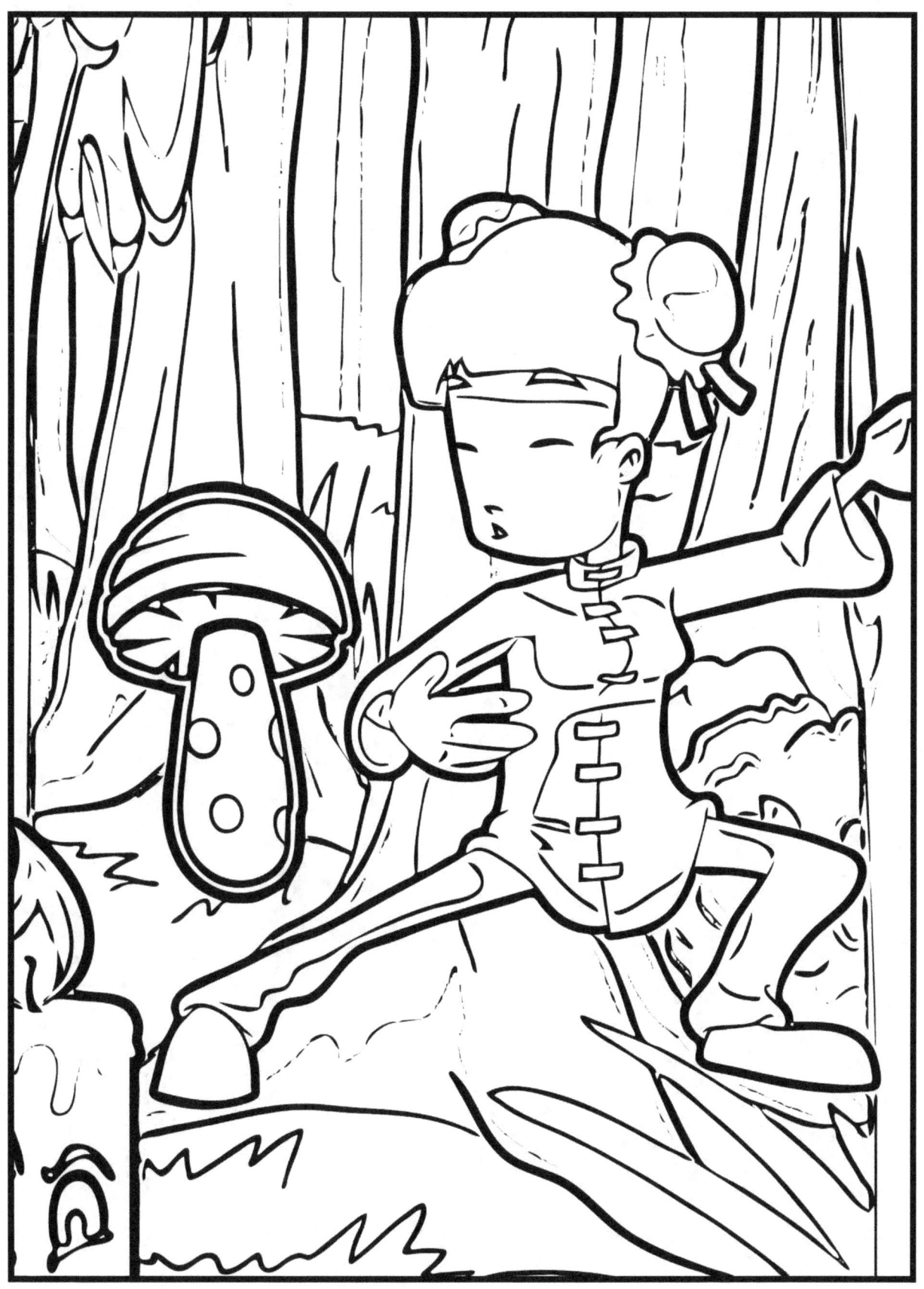

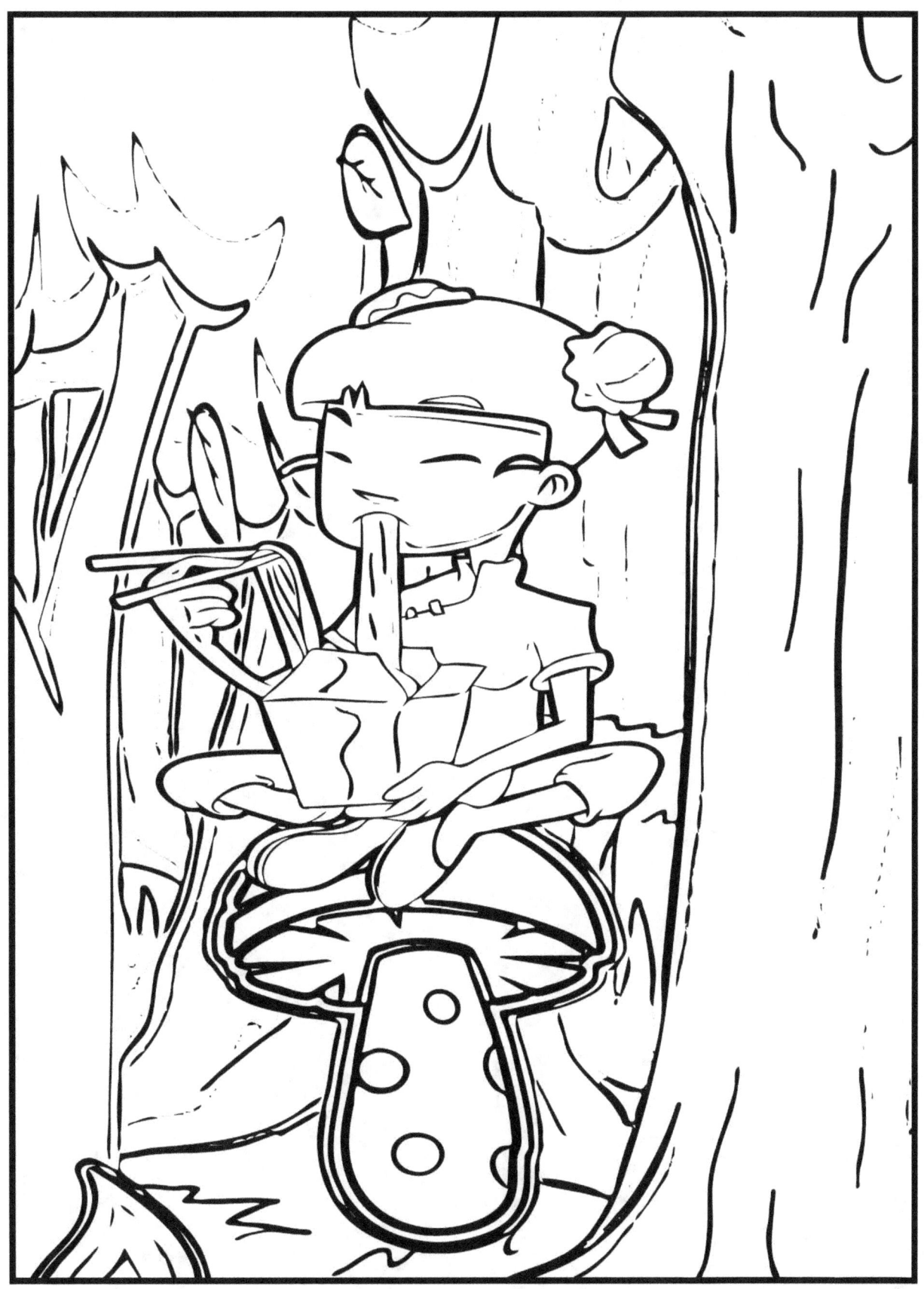

www.ingramcontent.com/pod-product-compliance
Lightning Source LLC
Chambersburg PA
CBHW081406170526
45166CB00010B/3228